T0062199

Mario Kart
Beginner's Guide

21st Century Skills **INNOVATION LIBRARY**

Josh Gregory

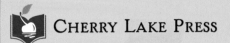
CHERRY LAKE PRESS

Published in the United States of America by Cherry Lake Publishing Group
Ann Arbor, Michigan
www.cherrylakepublishing.com

Reading Adviser: Beth Walker Gambro, MS, Ed., Reading Consultant, Yorkville, IL

Cherry Lake Press is an imprint of Cherry Lake Publishing Group.

Library of Congress Cataloging-in-Publication Data

Names: Gregory, Josh, author.
Title: Mario Kart : beginner's guide / by Josh Gregory.
Description: Ann Arbor, MI : Cherry Lake Publishing, 2022. | Series: 21st
  century skills innovation library | Includes bibliographical references
  and index. | Audience: Grades 4-6 | Summary: "The long-running Mario
  Kart series gives players the chance to zoom across some of Nintendo's
  most imaginative settings in high-speed races. This book's tips and
  strategies will have players speeding past the competition in no time.
  Includes table of contents, author biography, sidebars, glossary, index,
  and informative backmatter"— Provided by publisher.
Identifiers: LCCN 2021042754 (print) | LCCN 2021042755 (ebook) | ISBN
  9781534199699 (library binding) | ISBN 9781668900833 (paperback) | ISBN
  9781668902271 (ebook) | ISBN 9781668906590 (pdf)
Subjects: LCSH: Mario Kart Super Circuit (Game)—Juvenile literature.
Classification: LCC GV1469.35.M438 G74 2022 (print) | LCC GV1469.35.M438
  (ebook) | DDC 794.8—dc23
LC record available at https://lccn.loc.gov/2021042754
LC ebook record available at https://lccn.loc.gov/2021042755

Cherry Lake Publishing Group would like to acknowledge the work of the Partnership for 21st Century Learning, a Network of Battelle for Kids. Please visit http://www.battelleforkids.org/networks/p21 for more information.

Printed in the United States of America
Corporate Graphics

Josh Gregory is the author of more than 125 books for kids. He has written about everything from animals to technology to history. A graduate of the University of Missouri–Columbia, he currently lives in Chicago, Illinois.

Contents

CHAPTER 1

Speeding Through the Mushroom Kingdom

In 1992, the release of *Super Mario Kart* for the Super Nintendo Entertainment System (SNES) changed video games forever. The game had a simple concept. Using characters from the massively popular *Super Mario* series, it gave players the chance to compete in action-packed go-kart races. The race courses were all set in the Mushroom Kingdom, the colorful fantasy world of the *Mario* games. Along each route, players could pick up items such as turtle shells and banana peels and use them to **sabotage** other racers. The game's graphics and sense of speed were cutting edge at the time it was released. Like almost all SNES games, *Super Mario Kart* had two-dimensional (2D) graphics. But with the help of Nintendo's special Mode 7 technology, the game seemed like it moved in three dimensions.

Super Mario Kart quickly became a massive hit. Since then, many other games have been inspired by its fast-paced, easy-to-learn style. However, the *Mario Kart* series has remained the gold standard for fun, arcade-style racing games for 30 years. Each new sequel has added new features and improved on the classic gameplay. *Mario Kart 64* used true three-dimensional (3D) graphics, while *Mario Kart DS* was the first game in the series to let players race against each other online. Later games have also added characters and settings from all kinds of Nintendo series, from *Animal Crossing* to *Splatoon*.

The Villager from the *Animal Crossing* series is just one of many popular Nintendo characters to appear in *Mario Kart 8*.

Real-Life Racing

In 2020, Nintendo released one of the most unusual games in the *Mario Kart* series. *Mario Kart Live: Home Circuit* for the Switch puts players in control of real-life remote-controlled karts. Players build their own courses by arranging special marker devices around their homes. Then they control the action using a Switch. Cameras on the karts show the real-world course on the console's screen, with added computer graphics. This is an example of augmented reality (AR) technology. AR technology has also been used in popular games like *Pokemon GO*.

A new *Mario Kart* game has been released for almost every Nintendo game system. Each time, the new *Mario Kart* has been one of the system's best-selling games. There have also been spin-off games released for mobile devices, arcade machines, and more. Millions and millions of people have grown up with the series and then shared it with their own kids. People gather in groups to race together at parties. They also play it with friends online. They can play it at home or on the go. Sometimes, it seems like just about everyone on Earth has played a round of *Mario Kart* at one time or another!

Even though the graphics are a lot simpler, playing the original *Super Mario Kart* isn't all that different from playing the latest games in the series.

The latest game in the main *Mario Kart* series is *Mario Kart 8*. It was first released in 2014 for the Wii U console. While the game got great reviews, the Wii U was one of Nintendo's least-successful game consoles. This limited the game's audience. But Nintendo's next gaming system, the Switch, was a huge hit. Nintendo knew that a lot of Switch owners had never gotten the chance to play *Mario Kart 8*. They released a new and improved version of the game called *Mario Kart 8 Deluxe* in 2017. Since then, it has become the Switch's top-selling game, and one of the biggest selling games of all time.

One of the key reasons for *Mario Kart*'s success is that just about anyone can figure out how to play very quickly. The game's controls are always simple, and the object is usually just to reach the finish line before anyone else. Even people who almost never play video games can understand how it works. But that doesn't

If you press the + button while choosing your kart, you can turn on automatic steering by pressing L and automatic movement by pressing R. These options are helpful for people who have trouble handling too many buttons at once.

With a little practice, you'll be pulling off tricks such as attacking the racers behind you with shells.

mean *Mario Kart* is easy or boring. There are all kinds of skills and techniques that only the most experienced players will know how to pull off. Becoming an expert takes time and practice. But if you know just what to do, you'll be finishing in first sooner than you might expect.

CHAPTER 2

At the Starting Line

When you first start playing *Mario Kart 8*, the number of courses and modes might seem overwhelming at first. If you are playing the deluxe Switch version of the game, there are a total of 48 racecourses. If you want to truly excel at the game, you'll need to learn the ins and outs of each one. There are hidden shortcuts, unexpected obstacles, and other surprises in even the simplest courses. Some are fairly normal-looking tracks like you might see in a real-life race. Others are more like amusement park rides, only even more thrilling. You might find yourself driving through a world made of candy or a spooky haunted mansion. While most of the courses were created brand new for *Mario Kart 8*, there are also a bunch of classic courses from previous games in the series. Of course, even these courses have been updated with the latest graphics and a few new surprises.

Each of the 48 courses can be played in one of several modes. The first is called Grand Prix. In Grand Prix mode, you will choose among 12 events called cups. Each cup is made up of four consecutive races on a specific set of tracks. For each race, all the players will earn points depending on how they finish. Whoever finishes in first gets the most points. At the end of the four races, the player with the highest score wins. This means you don't necessarily have to win every race in a cup to get a first-place trophy. For

150		CONGRATULATIONS!	
1		Waluigi	52
2		Baby Daisy	48
3		Luigi	43
4		Link	36
5		Toadette	29
6		Donkey Kong	26
7		Wendy	22
8		Shy Guy	20
9		Rosalina	16
10		Lemmy	15
10		Dry Bowser	15
12		Baby Rosalina	6

Earning trophies in the Grand Prix events is one of the main goals of *Mario Kart 8*.

example, a player who comes in second place for all four races will end up with more points than someone who comes in first for two races and last for the other two.

In Time Trials mode, you simply pick a course and try to finish it as fast as you can. There won't be any

When racing against a Ghost, you'll see a somewhat see-through racer on the track. You can't attack this racer. You simply have to drive better to win!

other racers on the course to get in your way. If you have an especially good race, you can save a Ghost. This is a recording of your race. Later you can try racing against the Ghost to see if you can do even better. You can also post your Ghost online to challenge others players, or download other players' Ghosts to compete against.

A Different Way to Play

If you like the battling parts of the game more than the racing, you might want to give Battle mode a try. In this mode, players don't need to worry about the finish line. Instead, they drive around in an open arena and try to knock each other out using the game's many items. Each player's kart starts out with five balloons attached. When you get hit, you lose a balloon. The goal is to take out other players' balloons without losing your own.

Battle mode has its own set of arenas instead of the standard racing courses. These eight levels are more open. You can drive all over in any direction as you dodge attacks and try to catch other players off guard. Because Battle mode is so different from regular racing, even experienced *Mario Kart* players might need some practice before they are able to win regularly. However, this mode is a great way to add some variety if you ever need a break from racing.

Want to simply jump in and start racing against computer-controlled opponents? Select the VS Race mode. This mode lets you set all kinds of custom rules before you race. For example, you can change the difficulty of the computer-controlled racers or decide whether to allow attack items. This mode is a great way to practice different courses and improve your skills.

For most players, the real fun of *Mario Kart* comes from multiplayer action. If you are playing with friends on

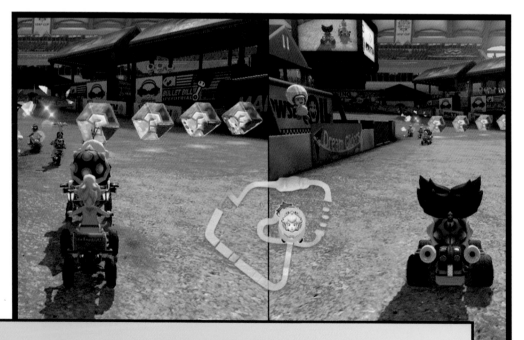

If you are playing with friends on one TV, the screen will be split up into separate sections for each player.

the same TV, all you need to do is choose Multiplayer from the game's main menu. Up to four players at a time can join in the fun. The rest of the racers will be computer-controlled. In Multiplayer, you can choose to either race a Grand Prix event or the VS Race mode. The other way to compete against human opponents is to play online. The competition can be very tough in online play. You could even find yourself matching up against some of the world's best *Mario Kart* players!

When starting a race you can choose between the options of 50cc, 100cc, 150cc, and 200cc. These numbers indicate the speed of the race. The higher the number, the faster everything goes. But keep in mind that higher speeds also mean higher difficulty. Beginners might want to play at 50cc, while 200cc is usually only for the most advanced players. If you want a good, balanced challenge, 150cc is probably the best speed to aim for.

Instead of choosing a speed, you can select the Mirror option. This flips a course around to a mirror image of its normal layout. If you think you know all of the tracks inside and out, this is a great way to add a new challenge.

CHAPTER 3

Behind the Wheel

So you've picked a mode, and you're ready to start racing. What happens next? The first thing you'll need to do is choose a character. Each character has different strengths and weaknesses. Some are faster, but harder to keep under control. Others are slow and heavy, but harder to knock off course. You can win with any of the characters. It all depends on what feels best to you, so practice to find the ones you like best.

After choosing a character, you'll get to select a vehicle. There are all kinds of different vehicle types, from motorcycles to standard go-karts. You'll also get to pick your vehicle's wheels and glider. These choices affect everything from your top speed to how easy it is to steer. Like choosing a character, these things are all up to you. Every player has different preferences.

Once a race begins, there are a few things you'll need to watch out for. *Mario Kart* isn't just a straightforward racing game. It also lets players attack each other as they zip around the courses. When you run into one of the colorful question mark boxes on a course, you will get a random item. You can carry up to two of these items at a time. After that, you will need to use one before you can pick up another. Some items are used to attack your rivals, while others give you benefits. They range from red turtle shells that lock on

Always aim for item boxes. Even if you don't need them, you might be able to prevent your opponents from getting them.

to other racers and knock them off course to mushrooms that give you a short burst of speed. The best way to get used to them is to simply practice and experiment to see what they do.

Each course also has a variety of special features that can help or hinder you. Most have ramps and speed-

Sometimes ramps are located off the beaten path of a course. These usually lead to shortcuts.

In addition to finding coins on the track, you can get them from item boxes.

boosting pads scattered around. Some might have obstacles that can smash your kart or send you spinning off the track. Tougher courses tend to have sections where you can fall off the sides. You won't be knocked out of the race, but you will lose precious time as your kart gets lifted back onto the track.

You'll also see coins scattered around on courses. Try to collect as many as you can. Each coin you grab

19

increases your speed, up to a total of 10 coins. Be careful, though. If you get hit by an item or fall off the track, you'll lose your coins and the speed boost.

The more you play *Mario Kart 8*, the bigger the game gets. You'll unlock all kinds of options for customizing your vehicle, and even new characters you can race as. How do you unlock these items? For the most part, it's all about collecting lots of coins. At first, every 50 coins you add to your total during races will unlock a new vehicle, wheels, or glider. Which item you get is random. After you've collected a total of 1,000 coins

Records of the Road

Interested in finding out how well you've been racing? On the main menu screen, select the small Play Stats icon in the bottom left corner. This will show you a wealth of information about how you play, including which character you use the most and the total distance you've driven in the game. You can also look up your record in online races and see a list of players you've recently raced against. It can be a lot of fun to check this info out. Do you have friends who play *Mario Kart*? Ask them to check out their stats sometime!

and unlocked 20 items, new items will only unlock for every 100 coins you collect. There are dozens of options to unlock. Some are mostly just interesting for their looks. Others can really affect the way your vehicle handles. Try out each new item as you unlock it, and don't forget to experiment with different combinations of vehicles, wheels, and gliders.

In the original *Mario Kart 8* for Wii U, many of the characters were hidden at first. To unlock them, players

Try a variety of combinations of kart pieces until you find the one that feels best to you. Some of them handle very differently from the others!

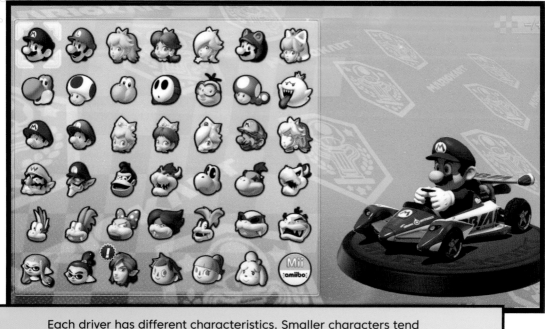

Each driver has different characteristics. Smaller characters tend to be lighter and faster, while bigger ones are heavier and tougher.

had to earn gold medals in the game's Grand Prix events. But in *Mario Kart 8 Deluxe*, almost all of the characters are available right from the start, with no unlocking needed. There is only one exception. You can unlock a special golden version of Mario himself by earning a gold medal in all of the Grand Prix events at the 200cc speed. It won't be easy!

You can also unlock special golden parts for your vehicle. The simplest one to get is the golden glider. All you need to do is collect a total of 10,000 coins. It'll take some time, but it's not a major challenge. To get the golden tires, you'll have to head to Time Trials mode and race against a series of Ghosts recorded by the game's creators. Beat them all to get your new tires. Finally, if you want to unlock a golden kart, you'll have to become a Grand Prix expert. You'll need to finish every cup in both 150cc and mirror versions. Not only will you need gold trophies for all of these, but you'll also need to unlock the tiny star that displays next to the trophy. To do this, you'll need a final score of at least 55 points for each one.

CHAPTER 4

Going for Gold

Feel like you've got a good handle on the basics of *Mario Kart 8*? There's still plenty more you can do to up your game.

Want a little boost right at the start of a race? Start **accelerating** at just the right moment as the game counts down to the start of the race. Press and hold the button right as the number two stops moving on the countdown. Keep holding it and you will blast off from the starting line as soon as the race begins. It takes a little practice to get the timing just right. But if you are close, you'll still get a smaller speed boost even if your timing isn't perfect.

Perhaps the most important skill you can learn in *Mario Kart* is **drifting** around corners. This is a technique that sends your vehicle sliding sideways, allowing you to make tight turns at high speeds. You'll also get a pretty good speed boost as you come out of the drift and straighten out control of your vehicle. The speed boost depends on how long you've been drifting. This means you should try to make long drifts around corners as often as you can.

There are three possible levels of drift boost. As you hold down the drift button, you'll see colored sparks start coming from the bottom of your vehicle. These

Pay attention to the sparks coming off your tires to see if you are drifting correctly.

sparks show you which drift boost you have reached. At first, the sparks will be blue. After a while, they will turn orange. Finally, they will turn purple. This is how you know you've reached the maximum level of drift boost. Not every curve or corner will give you enough time to reach this third level. You might have to settle for ending your drift at the first or second level to avoid

If you fall out of bounds of a course, a character named Lakitu will come and drag you back on track with a fishing pole.

You'll know you timed your jump correctly at the top of a ramp if your character does a stunt in the air.

slamming into a wall. It will take some time to get a feel for drifting. But eventually it will become second nature.

If you tap the drift button without holding it, your vehicle will do a short hop into the air. You can use this to get a little burst of extra speed each time you hit a ramp. Just as your vehicle reaches the end of the ramp, tap the drift button. Your character will do a trick and get a small speed bonus.

Looking for even more chances for speed boosts? Try driving directly behind any racer who's in front of you. After a short time, you'll see a whooshing wind effect and get a boost. Use this opportunity to swerve around and pass the driver you were tailgating!

Another thing you should consider carefully is when and where to use different items. Good item management strategy can make or break a race. If you are near the front of the pack, consider playing

Racing into the Future

What's in store for the *Mario Kart* series? No one is really sure, outside of maybe the developers at Nintendo, and they're very good at keeping secrets. In the meantime, fans have been left to make their best guesses about what will happen next. Some think *Mario Kart 8* is so good that it will be a long time before Nintendo needs to make a sequel. They argue that it would be better to simply release new courses for the existing game. On the other hand, Nintendo has almost always made new *Mario Kart* games for each of its game systems. Because they are bound to create a new game console at some point, it's likely there will one day be a brand new *Mario Kart* to go with it. If things go like they have in the past, the series will only continue to get more popular going forward!

Holding an item behind you is an important strategy to master if you are near the front of the pack.

defensively. Items such as the banana peel and single turtle shells can be held behind your vehicle to act as a shield against attacks. To do this, hold down the item button instead of tapping it. If you let go of the button, you will use the item and lose your defense.

The closer a racer is to last place, the better the chance they have of getting the most powerful items.

This means the players at the front are very vulnerable to attacks from behind. For example, the notorious blue turtle shell can zoom from anywhere on the course to seek out the player in first place. One way to avoid this attack is to deliberately stay in second place until the race is almost over. This is a risky move, so be sure you have the skills to launch into first place when you're ready!

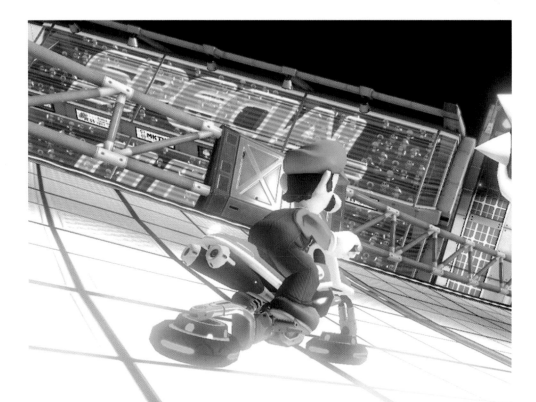

Even if you are coasting toward victory with a wide lead, a blue shell can completely wreck your chances of winning a race.

Much of your success in *Mario Kart* will come down to getting a feel for the controls and learning the courses. In other words, it takes plenty of practice! And even the best players don't win every time. There will always be races where you get unlucky with items, or where you get hit with a turtle shell right as you are about to cross the finish line. But this is all part of the fun of *Mario Kart*. Remember that the point of playing isn't just to win. It's to have fun! Laugh off mistakes and bad luck. There's always another race ahead of you!

GLOSSARY

accelerating (ak-SELL-ur-ate-ing) increasing speed

augmented reality (awg-MEN-tid ree-AL-uh-tee) interactive digital experiences that take place in a real-world environment

developers (dih-VEL-uh-purz) people who make video games or other computer programs

drifting (DRIF-ting) a way of turning a car that involves locking the tires and making them slide along the ground

sabotage (SAB-uh-tahj) intentionally ruining someone's ability to do something

FIND OUT MORE

Books

Cunningham, Kevin. *Video Game Designer*. Ann Arbor, MI: Cherry Lake Publishing, 2016.

Loh-Hagan, Virginia. *Video Games*. Ann Arbor, MI: Cherry Lake Publishing, 2021.

Powell, Marie. *Asking Questions About Video Games*. Ann Arbor, MI: Cherry Lake Publishing, 2016.

Websites

Mario Kart 8 for Nintendo Switch - Official Site
https://mariokart8.nintendo.com/
Check out videos and learn about the features of *Mario Kart 8* at the official site.

Tech Evolution: 25 Years of Super Mario Kart
https://www.eurogamer.net/articles/digitalfoundry-2017-tech-evolution-25-years-of-super-mario-kart
Learn more about the history of the *Mario Kart* series.

INDEX